FOOD
SAFETY BASICS

by Carolee Laine

Content Consultant
Meghan Ames, MSPH, RD, LDN
Research Nutritionist
John Hopkins School of Medicine

Core Library

An Imprint of Abdo Publishing
abdopublishing.com

abdopublishing.com

Published by Abdo Publishing, a division of ABDO, PO Box 398166, Minneapolis, Minnesota 55439. Copyright © 2016 by Abdo Consulting Group, Inc. International copyrights reserved in all countries. No part of this book may be reproduced in any form without written permission from the publisher. Core Library™ is a trademark and logo of Abdo Publishing.

Printed in the United States of America, North Mankato, Minnesota
042015
092015

Cover Photo: Vika Valter/iStockphoto
Interior Photos: Vika Valter/iStockphoto, 1; iStockphoto, 4, 26, 34; S.D. Butcher & Son/Library of Congress, 7; Library of Congress, 10; BSIP/Newscom, 12; Shutterstock Images, 15, 17, 45; US Department of Agriculture, 20, 38; US Food and Drug Administration/Food Standards Committee, 23; Zeljko Radojko/Shutterstock Images, 29; Red Line Editorial, 32

Editor: Mirella Miller
Series Designer: Becky Daum

Library of Congress Control Number: 2015931972

Cataloging-in-Publication Data
Laine, Carolee.
 Food safety basics / Carolee Laine.
   p. cm. -- (Food matters)
Includes bibliographical references and index.
ISBN 978-1-62403-863-1
1. Food--safety measures--Juvenile literature. 2. Food contamination--Juvenile literature.   I. Title.
363.19--dc23
                                                    2015931972

CONTENTS

CHAPTER ONE

HISTORY OF FOOD SAFETY

You have just come home from school. The first thing you do is head to the refrigerator for some cold milk. You start to fill up your glass. Wait! What's that terrible odor? Your nose tells you the milk is not fresh. Will you drink it? Of course not! You know spoiled milk is not safe to drink.

Early people learned about food safety the hard way. They ate or drank foods that had spoiled, and

Food safety guidelines have developed over thousands of years as scientists learn more about foods.

they became sick. Thousands of years ago, people began searching for ways to preserve foods to keep them fresh and safe. The concern for food safety continued throughout history. Now government agencies are responsible for food safety throughout the worldwide food industry.

Keep It Dry

Early people in many parts of the world preserved foods by drying them. Ancient Egyptians built silos, or storage tanks, to hold large quantities of dry grain. Ancient Romans dried food by salting it.

Native Americans braided together the husks of several ears of corn and hung them over tree branches or poles to dry in the wind. Today scientists know the water in moist foods can enable harmful substances, such as bacteria, yeasts, and molds, to multiply and make people sick. Early people learned that removing moisture from foods makes them last longer.

Native Americans dried fish and meat to keep them fresh longer.

Keep It Cold

Some foods must be kept cold to slow the growth of germs that can make people sick. Early people living in cold climates preserved foods by packing them in snow or leaving them outside to freeze. In warmer regions, people harvested blocks of ice from frozen lakes in winter. They stored the ice in insulated icehouses so it could be used during other seasons. Packing foods in ice helps keep them fresh and safe from harmful microorganisms.

The invention of refrigerators in the 1800s transformed food safety. Meat packers no longer had to rely on natural ice to keep their products from spoiling. Refrigerated railroad cars began transporting fresh foods to widespread markets. In the early 1900s, refrigerators were developed for household use. By the 1930s, an electric refrigerator was a common appliance in kitchens across the United States. By the 1950s, more than 90 percent of US homes had a refrigerator.

Heat It

Another important development in food safety came about because of milk. Raw

What's an Icebox?

An icebox was an early home refrigerator. It was a wooden chest lined with metal and insulated with sawdust or seaweed. A large block of ice placed inside the box kept foods cold—until the ice melted. A pan that collected water from the melted ice had to be emptied regularly. Ice wagons brought ice directly to homes. A sign placed in the window let the iceman know a delivery was needed. Iceboxes did not maintain a consistent temperature, but they still helped to prevent foods from spoiling.

milk, or milk used directly from a cow without processing, was a source of many illnesses. People discovered that boiling milk helped prevent illnesses. However, boiling also changed the taste of the milk in a way some people did not like.

In the 1860s, a French scientist named Louis Pasteur developed a process to keep wine from spoiling. Pasteur discovered that heating wine preserved it without destroying its taste. People began using this process, which became known as pasteurization,

Many Americans in the 1940s canned the fruits and vegetables grown in their gardens.

to treat raw milk. It greatly reduced illnesses. Laws requiring the pasteurization of milk were put into effect in the early 1900s.

Preserve It

Heat is important to food safety in other ways as well. Using heat to cook some foods makes them taste better. It also makes them safe to eat. Eating raw hamburger or a raw egg could make you sick. But a juicy grilled burger or hard-boiled eggs make a delicious lunch.

Some foods, such as vegetables or fruits, do not have to be cooked. However, these foods do not remain fresh for very long. People learned to preserve these foods by canning them. The canning process involves placing fresh foods in cans or jars and heating them. When the cans or jars are cooled, a seal is formed. This seal helps keep the foods safe to eat.

Food safety remains a major concern. Understanding how foods can make people sick is important. How is the safety of the food supply protected today? Learning these things and more can help ensure food safety in your home and school.

EXPLORE ONLINE

Chapter One mentions how some people in the early 1900s disagreed with the need to pasteurize milk. The website below focuses on the continuing debate over food safety and raw milk. As you know, every source is different. How is the information given in the website different from the information in this chapter? What information is the same? How do the two sources present information differently? What can you learn from this website?

Food Safety and Raw Milk

mycorelibrary.com/food-safety-basics

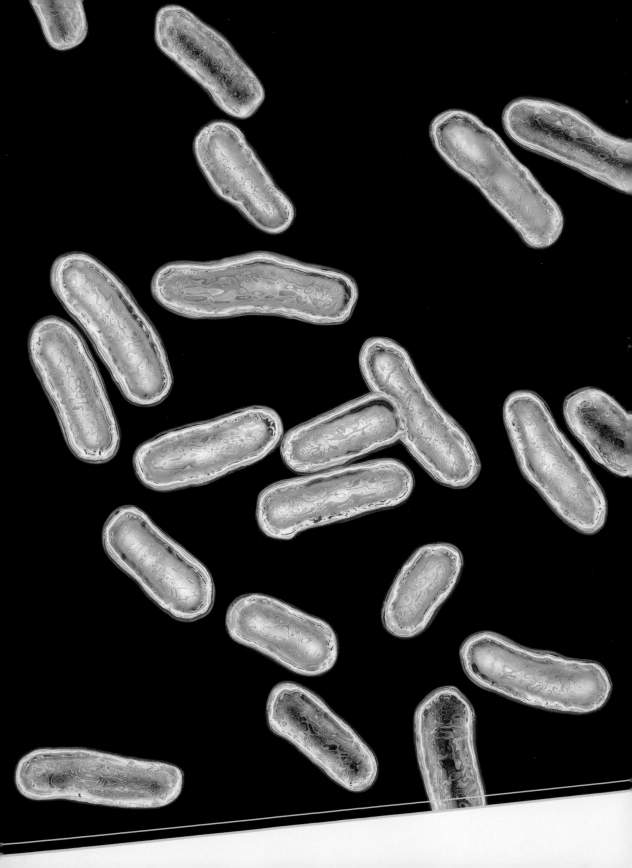

CHAPTER TWO

WHAT YOU EAT CAN MAKE YOU SICK

Every year approximately 48 million people in the United States get sick from something they ate. That is one in six Americans! A foodborne illness generally lasts only a short time, and people recover quickly. In some cases, however, people must receive treatment in a hospital. Severe cases of foodborne illnesses result in approximately 3,000 deaths in the United States each year.

Salmonella is one common bacteria that is responsible for many cases of foodborne illness in the United States each year.

Anyone can get a foodborne illness, but some groups of people are more likely to suffer serious results. These groups include babies, young children, elderly people, and people with certain health problems. Foodborne illness is a public health issue.

How do foods make people sick, and why is food safety an important concern?

How Do Foods Make People Sick?

The digestive tract is the part of the body that breaks down foods. An infection in the digestive tract makes a person sick. Most foodborne illnesses are caused by harmful bacteria. These

Good Bacteria

Not all bacteria are bad. Some bacteria are helpful to people. Good bacteria help people digest foods and fight infection. These good bacteria live in the digestive system, on the skin, and in the mouth. Without good bacteria, people would die. Foods such as yogurt and cheese owe their taste and texture to good bacteria. These foods may even improve the health of some people. Some types of good bacteria are also used to produce chocolate, coffee, vinegar, wine, and sausage.

Eggs are one food that can contain harmful bacteria.

tiny organisms cause infections that lead to sickness. Bacteria can multiply quickly in warm, moist places, such as the digestive tract.

A person with a foodborne illness may suffer stomach pain, vomiting, diarrhea, fever, and chills. In mild cases, these symptoms may last from a few hours to several days. In severe cases, a person will require a doctor's care and may need to be treated in a hospital. In extreme cases, foodborne illness can be fatal.

Why Do Some Foods Make People Sick?

Harmful bacteria may be found in many types of raw foods, including meat, poultry, fish, shellfish, eggs, dairy products, fruits, and vegetables. Foods infected with harmful bacteria may not look or smell different from other foods. But people who eat these foods may become sick.

Thorough cooking destroys harmful bacteria

People who work with food must wash their hands often.

in foods, and freezing can stop the spread of harmful bacteria. These methods can help keep bacteria at safe levels so they do not cause illness. Hot foods should be kept above 140°F (60°C), and cold foods should be kept below 40°F (4°C). When foods' temperatures are in the danger zone—between 40°F and 140°F (4°C and 60°C)—bacteria can multiply, increasing the chances of foodborne illness.

If food preparers are not careful about cleanliness, harmful bacteria can spread from one food to another through a process called cross-contamination. People who handle foods must wash their hands, kitchen utensils, and kitchen surfaces to prevent the spread of bacteria that can cause foodborne illnesses.

Viruses cause some foodborne illnesses. Viruses are even smaller than bacteria, and they cause infections in people or animals. Food preparers who are infected with a virus or bacteria can spread that sickness by handling foods without washing their hands thoroughly.

Outbreaks of Foodborne Illnesses

A foodborne illness outbreak occurs when a group of people eat the same contaminated foods and two or more of them come down with the same illness. Sometimes an outbreak happens when people attend a picnic or a party and eat foods that were left out at room temperature for several hours. Some outbreaks can be traced to a local restaurant where foods were contaminated by a sick employee or were not handled properly.

Date	Food Source	Number of People Who Became Ill	Number of Deaths
2002	Deli turkey meat	Approximately 50 people in 7 states	8
2006	Spinach	Approximately 200 people in 26 states	3
2008	Jalapeño peppers	Approximately 1,500 people in 42 states	2
2008–2009	Peanut butter	Approximately 700 people in 46 states	9
2011	Cantaloupes	Approximately 150 people in 28 states	30

Selected Outbreaks of Foodborne Illnesses

How does the information in the table support what you have learned from the text about outbreaks of foodborne illnesses? What new information does the table provide? How does the table increase your understanding of foodborne illness outbreaks?

In some cases, people in many communities across several states have become sick with the same foodborne illness. These widespread outbreaks have been traced to foods that were contaminated by growers or processors in one part of the country and shipped to many other locations.

CHAPTER THREE

WHO KEEPS OUR FOODS SAFE?

n 1862 President Abraham Lincoln signed a law
that created the United States Department of
Agriculture (USDA). The USDA became responsible
for managing the country's farming issues. It collected
and published information about crops. It also tested
soils and provided advice to farmers. Over time the
government's role in protecting food safety began
to expand.

President Abraham Lincoln created the USDA to help with
food safety.

In the late 1800s and early 1900s, the responsibilities of the USDA increased. It began developing standards for food processing. The organization also prevented diseased animals from being used as foods. To keep our nation's food supply safe, the USDA regulated the importing and exporting of animals and meat products.

Regulation of other foods and drugs was left to the states. Each state had different rules. To provide better control, the government passed additional laws to make food products safe, and

The Jungle

In 1906 Upton Sinclair published *The Jungle*, a book about immigrants who worked in the meatpacking industry in Chicago, Illinois. Sinclair described the dirty conditions and bad practices that made meat products unsafe for people to eat. Although the story is fiction, the descriptions of the meatpacking industry of the early 1900s are factual. Readers were outraged and demanded reform. The result was the Pure Food and Drug Act of 1906, which led to the regulation of food processing in the United States.

The Food Standards Committee meets in 1930 after the creation of the US Food and Drug Administration (FDA).

it created agencies to enforce these laws. In 1930 the agency that protects the safety of food products and medicines became known as the US Food and Drug Administration (FDA).

During the 1950s and 1960s, the government passed laws to regulate the use of chemicals added to foods. Responsibility for enforcing these laws through inspections was transferred in 1981 to the Food and Safety Inspection Service (FSIS).

Food Safety Today

The USDA, the FDA, and the FSIS are responsible for the safety of the US food supply today. Some of their responsibilities overlap. The USDA is responsible for the safety of meat, poultry, and certain egg products. The FDA is responsible for all other foods, as well as medicines. The FSIS ensures meats, poultry, and egg products are safe. Through inspections of processing centers, the FSIS ensures proper handling and packaging of foods. The FSIS and the FDA also regulate proper labeling of foods. This ensures food labels contain accurate information. Federal, state, and local governments work together to ensure the safety of foods.

Before writing *The Jungle*, Upton Sinclair investigated the meatpacking industry in Chicago. He found many problems that threatened food safety. In 1906 Sinclair wrote a letter to President Theodore Roosevelt. In the letter, Sinclair urged the president to send government inspectors to Chicago. He wrote:

> *Inspection to be effective should include the entire twenty-four hours. . . . The railroads and express companies bring animals into the city every hour in the day. When [an inspector] has access to every room in the packing houses and knows what is done there every hour in the twenty-four; . . . when he knows the destination and use of the refuse which the meat and liver wagons gather after nightfall . . . when he knows the meat that comes to the city by wagon and other ways, then . . . he can give something like an accurate estimation of the amount of diseased, putrid meat that is converted into meat in Chicago.*

Source: Upton Sinclair. "Letter to President Theodore Roosevelt." National Archives. *The US National Archives and Records Administration*, March 10, 1906. Web. Accessed October 6, 2014.

What's the Big Idea?

What was Sinclair's reason for wanting the government to inspect the meatpacking industry? Did Sinclair expect the meatpackers to cooperate with an investigation? Find two details in the letter to support your answer.

CHAPTER FOUR

FOOD SAFETY IS EVERYONE'S BUSINESS

Many people are involved in providing foods for people to eat. Farmers grow crops or raise animals that are sources of food. Processors put foods in cans, boxes, or packages for freezing. Truck drivers transport foods to markets. Grocers store and sell foods, which people buy and cook to eat at home. Cooks prepare and serve foods in restaurants. Everyone is responsible for food safety

Each person who handles food is responsible for the food's safety.

Organic Foods

Organic foods contain ingredients produced without the use of pesticides or fertilizers. Organic meats, poultry, eggs, and dairy products come from animals that eat organic feed. Some consumers believe foods are safer and taste better if they are produced without the use of chemicals. They also believe organic foods have more vitamins and other nutrients. Before foods can be sold as organic, farms must be inspected to determine if farmers are following the rules established by the USDA National Organic Program. Companies that process organic foods must also meet government standards.

in the farm-to-table food chain.

Food Producers

Food safety begins at the source. To provide a good harvest, farmers use fertilizers to help crops grow. They must make sure fertilizers do not contain harmful substances that would make foods unsafe for people to eat. Farmers must follow guidelines from the Environmental Protection Agency (EPA) for the safe use of pesticides.

Some farmers raise chickens, hogs, milk

Farm animals must be kept healthy so the foods they provide are safe for people to eat.

cows, or beef cattle. The USDA provides standards for farmers who raise animals as a food source. These standards include feeding animals a proper diet. USDA inspectors also oversee the process of butchering animals to ensure proper treatment of the animals, as well as delivery of meat products.

Food Processors and Transporters

In any factory that cans, freezes, or packages foods, workers must follow very strict rules about cleanliness. The FSIS provides regulations and inspects factories. Workers must wash their hands often and wear protective clothing to prevent contaminating foods.

Most foods in the United States are transported by truck. But trains, airplanes, and ships are also part of the farm-to-table food chain. The FDA provides regularly updated rules for transporting foods. They outline how equipment should be cleaned, as well as the proper temperatures at which foods must be stored and the lengths of time foods can be kept to prevent them from spoiling.

Grocery Stores and Restaurants

Grocery stores are responsible for food safety. Places that sell fresh foods can attract rodents and insects that spread diseases, so cleanliness and pest control are essential. Workers who handle foods must follow food safety guidelines. They must examine produce frequently to make sure only fresh fruits and vegetables are available for sale. Frozen and refrigerated foods must be kept at the proper temperatures.

Restaurant owners face similar challenges as grocery stores do with cleanliness and pest control. They must store and cook foods at proper temperatures and serve foods promptly. Many states require restaurant workers to get a food handler certificate by passing a test about food safety.

The FDA publishes the *Food Code*, which contains standards for

YOUR LIFE
Packing School Lunches

Do you take your lunch to school? You may eat lunch several hours after you get to school. Here are some ways to keep your lunch tasty and safe until you are ready to eat it. Keep your lunch in the refrigerator until you leave for school. Be sure to use an insulated lunch box. Pack a frozen drink box or bottle next to foods that should be kept cold. Keep your lunch box out of direct sunlight and away from heat until it is time to eat.

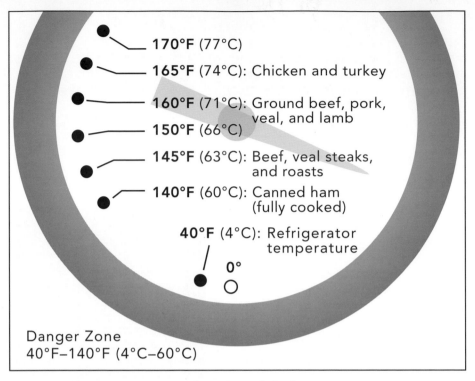

170°F (77°C)

165°F (74°C): Chicken and turkey

160°F (71°C): Ground beef, pork, veal, and lamb

150°F (66°C)

145°F (63°C): Beef, veal steaks, and roasts

140°F (60°C): Canned ham (fully cooked)

40°F (4°C): Refrigerator temperature

0°

Danger Zone
40°F–140°F (4°C–60°C)

Proper Temperatures for Food Safety

A thermometer is an instrument for measuring temperature. How does this illustration of a thermometer help you understand the connection between temperature and food safety?

grocery stores and restaurants. The code covers training of food workers and procedures for food inspections. Local agencies, such as county health departments and city health inspectors, enforce the standards in the code.

Secretary of Agriculture Tom Vilsack delivered the following speech in honor of the 150th anniversary of the USDA. He said:

> In 2012, USDA will commemorate and celebrate the 150th anniversary of our founding in 1862, when President Abraham Lincoln signed into law an act of Congress establishing the United States Department of Agriculture.
>
> Two and one-half years later, in what would be his final annual message to the Congress, Lincoln called USDA "The People's Department." At that time, about half of all Americans lived on farms, compared with about 2 percent today. But through our work on food, agriculture, economic development, science, natural resource conservation and a host of issues, USDA still fulfills Lincoln's vision—touching the lives of every American, every day.

Source: Tom Vilsack. "Message from Secretary Vilsack about USDA 150th." United States Department of Agriculture. USDA.gov, 2015. Web. Accessed October 1, 2014.

Point of View

After reading Tom Vilsack's speech, reread Upton Sinclair's letter in Chapter Three. What is the point of view of each author? How are these two authors' points of view similar? How are they different? Write a paragraph comparing the two points of view reflected in the letter and the speech.

KEEPING FOODS SAFE

Food safety is everyone's business. Farmers, truck drivers, food processors, grocers, and cooks all play a role in keeping foods safe. Consumers play a role too. Learning what you and your family can do to keep foods safe is important. The following tools will help keep you from getting sick from unsafe food.

It helps to keep foods safe and organize your grocery shopping list by the types of food you need to buy.

Shopping for Foods

At the grocery store, put canned and packaged foods in the shopping cart first. Examine fresh foods, such as fruits and vegetables. Avoid selecting any with dark spots or broken skin. Look at the expiration date on packaged meat, poultry, fish, and dairy products. Do not buy foods that will expire before you have time to eat them. Examine eggs to make sure the shells are not cracked.

Place frozen and refrigerated foods in the shopping cart last. At the checkout, meats should be bagged separately from fruits and vegetables. Juices from raw meats contain harmful

Understand Product Dating

Product dating provides guidelines for buying and using foods. A "sell by" date tells stores how long to display foods for sale. Consumers should buy foods before the date on the label. A "use by" date is the last date recommended for using foods. A "best if used before" date indicates when foods have the best flavor or quality. Foods might be safe to eat after this date, but they may not taste or look as good.

bacteria such as E. coli, salmonella, and listeria. If meat packages leak, the juices could contaminate other foods. Foods should not be bagged with nonfood items, such as household cleaners. Take foods home as soon as possible. If you have a long drive or it is hot outside, take a cooler with you.

Storing Foods

Storing foods properly is key to controlling the growth of bacteria and other germs that can make people sick. Most meat, poultry, or fish should be put in the freezer, but it can be kept in the refrigerator if it is going to be cooked within two days. Eggs should be stored in the carton on a refrigerator shelf. Some fruits, such as berries, and some vegetables, such as lettuce and cucumbers, require refrigeration. Store fruits and vegetables in separate drawers inside the refrigerator. Do not store them next to raw meat, which could cause cross-contamination. Any fruits or vegetables that have been peeled or cut should

Storing food properly in the refrigerator will help it last longer and stay safe to eat.

be refrigerated. Apples, potatoes, and tomatoes are some foods that can be stored at room temperature.

Before eating or cooking any fruits or vegetables, wash them thoroughly under running water. This removes some of the dirt, pesticides, or bacteria on the outside of these foods.

Refrigerating or freezing foods can slow, but not stop, the growth of bacteria. Time is an important factor in food safety. Put frozen and refrigerated foods away immediately after returning from the grocery store. Leaving them at room temperature allows bacteria to grow. Remember spoiled foods do not necessarily look or smell bad, so other precautions must be taken to keep foods safe.

Leftovers should be put in the refrigerator or freezer as soon as possible. Refrigerate leftovers in containers with tight lids, or wrap them in foil or plastic wrap. Freeze leftovers in plastic containers, plastic bags, or foil. Label them with a date and use them within three to four months.

Preparing and Cooking Foods

Thaw frozen foods safely in the refrigerator—never at room temperature. After preparing raw meat, poultry, and fish, wash your hands, utensils, and cutting boards. This will prevent juices that contain harmful bacteria from contaminating other foods.

Cook foods to the proper temperature on the stove or in the oven. Color, moistness, or texture can help you tell if foods are properly cooked. The use of a cooking thermometer is the best way to ensure meat, poultry, or casseroles are safe to eat. Some thermometers are inserted before foods are cooked. Others are used to test foods as they are cooking.

Paying Attention to Food Recalls

A food recall occurs when a producer, processor, or government agency believes a certain type of food may make people sick. Sometimes foods are recalled because they are contaminated by harmful bacteria. Recalled foods are removed from grocery store shelves.

Large recalls are generally published in newspapers or announced on television and radio. Notices of smaller recalls can be found on the FDA or USDA websites. The notices indicate the brand of food and the dates and locations where it was sold. Throw away any foods that have been recalled.

FURTHER EVIDENCE

Chapter Five has a great deal of information about ways you can keep foods safe. What is one of the chapter's main points? What evidence in the chapter supports this main point? Go to the website below. Choose a quote from the website that supports a main point in the chapter. Write a few sentences explaining how the quote you chose relates to this chapter.

Fight BAC!
mycorelibrary.com/food-safety-basics

- Most foodborne illnesses are mild, but outbreaks caused by contaminated foods can affect hundreds of people in many locations.
- Cooking or storing foods at proper temperatures can slow the growth of harmful germs, and cleanliness can reduce the spread of harmful bacteria.
- The USDA, the FDA, the FSIS, and state and local health departments are responsible for food safety.
- Government agencies provide rules and guidelines for farmers, truck drivers, food processors, grocers, and cooks to protect the safety of foods in every step of the farm-to-table food chain.
- Consumers can protect food safety by shopping wisely and preparing and cooking foods properly.
- Food recalls prevent the spread of foodborne illnesses by removing contaminated foods from grocery shelves and alerting consumers to the dangers of eating these foods.

IN THE KITCHEN

Strawberry Freezer Jam

- Six 8-ounce glass jars with lids and bands
- 4 cups crushed strawberries
- 3 cups sugar
- 1 box low- or no-sugar pectin
- 1 cup water

Rinse the berries in cold water. Ask an adult to cut off the stems and leaves. Mash the strawberries with a potato masher or using a blender or food processor. Put the sugar into a large saucepan and stir in the pectin. Then add the water. Ask an adult to bring the mixture to a boil over medium heat and stir constantly for one minute. Remove the mixture from the heat and quickly add the crushed strawberries. Stir for one minute or until mixed well. Spoon the jam into the jars, leaving one inch at the top for the jam to expand during freezing. Put the lids and bands on the jars and place the jars in the refrigerator for about 24 hours or until the jam is set. Store the jam in the refrigerator for up to three weeks or in the freezer for up to one year.

Another View

In Chapter Four you read about organic foods. People have different opinions about this topic. Ask an adult, such as a librarian, to help you find sources about organic foods. Write a short essay comparing and contrasting opposing views about organic foods. Which point of view do you support? Explain why.

Take a Stand

This book discusses the importance of cleanliness. It explains how food safety is everyone's responsibility. Suppose a restaurant owner discovers an employee is not following guidelines for cleanliness. What do you think the owner should do? Give a reason for your answer. Support your reason with facts and details from this book.

Say What?

Learning about food safety can involve a great deal of new vocabulary. Find five new words you learned in this book. Write the meanings in your own words. Use each word in a new sentence.

Dig Deeper

After reading this book, what questions do you still have about food safety? Write one or two questions to guide your research. With an adult's help, find a few reliable sources to help answer your questions. Write a paragraph explaining what you learned from each source.

GLOSSARY

bacteria
tiny organisms that can cause people to become sick

contaminated
exposed to something harmful

fertilizers
substances that are added to soil and help plants grow

foodborne illness
a sickness caused by eating food or drinking a beverage that is not safe

infection
a disease caused by harmful bacteria or viruses

organic
containing ingredients raised or grown without the use of chemicals

outbreak
an event, such as a foodborne illness, that affects many people

pasteurization
the process of heating a liquid to make it safe to drink

pesticides
chemicals used to kill harmful insects

raw milk
milk used directly from a cow and without pasteurization

regulation
a rule

viruses
very tiny organisms that cause diseases in humans or animals

LEARN MORE

Books

Friedman, Lauri S., ed. *Organic Food and Farming.* Detroit: Greenhaven Press, 2010.

Petrie, Kristin. *Food Safety: Avoiding Hidden Dangers.* Minneapolis: Abdo Publishing, 2012.

Rissman, Rebecca. *Eating Organic.* Minneapolis: Abdo Publishing, 2016.

Websites

To learn more about Food Matters, visit **booklinks.abdopublishing.com**. These links are routinely monitored and updated to provide the most current information available.

Visit **mycorelibrary.com** for free additional tools for teachers and students.

INDEX

ABOUT THE AUTHOR

Carolee Laine is an educator and children's writer. She has written social studies textbooks and other educational materials. Laine lives in the Chicago suburbs.